EAST HAM
AND WEST HAM
TRAMWAYS

Robert J Harley

MP Middleton Press

Cover Picture: The date is 1928 and the crew of West Ham car 66 snatch a break at Stratford Broadway before the return journey to East Ham Town Hall. Service 1 operated over the tracks of both corporations. (G.N.Southerden)

Cover colours: These are similar to the later livery of West Ham Corporation Tramways.

First published April 1995

ISBN 1 873793 52 9

© Middleton Press 1995

Design - Deborah Goodridge

Published by Middleton Press
            Easebourne Lane
            Midhurst
            West Sussex
            GU29 9AZ
            Tel: 01730 813169

Printed & bound by Biddles Ltd,
            Guildford and Kings Lynn

PART 1 - EAST HAM TRAMWAYS

PART 2 - WEST HAM TRAMWAYS

INTRODUCTION AND ACKNOWLEDGEMENTS

This volume of the Tramways Classics series aims to present a picture of two hard working tramway systems which supplied cheap and efficient local transport. Scenes from the past invite nostalgia, and I hope also that the reader will be reminded of the dedicated public service of the tram crews, maintenance and office staff. Their efforts ensured that municipal enterprise reached a level of excellence, which was seldom matched after the trams disappeared.

My own introduction to the area covered in this book came in the late 1950s long after the trams had finished. Once a month I accompanied my father on a Saturday morning jaunt to Romford from our home in South East London. The trip involved crossing the Thames on the Woolwich Ferry, then we changed to the 101 bus for a ride past the docks, through East Ham town centre and out to Manor Park Station. There we took an electric train to complete our journey. The roads around East Ham were very much trolleybus territory in those days and subsequent investigation into the neighbouring borough of West Ham revealed a maze of small streets many still retaining the granite sett surface left over from the tramway era. Gaps in the rows of terraced houses served as a reminder of the recent wartime bombing,

and there was much talk of redevelopment, new shops and houses, and above all a "modern" road system to cater for the increasing numbers of private motorists. The trolleybuses, like the trams before them, did not fit into this scheme of things and as often happens in the field of human endeavour, many other positive aspects of community life were jettisoned in a mad dash to reach the future.

The pictures contained in this album depict a vanished age; some locations have simply disappeared to be swallowed up by swathes of concrete and steel. Although life was hard in the first half of the twentieth century, the sense of community was strong, and whilst there may be no romance in poverty, thirty years of tower blocks, hideous architecture, fume ridden traffic schemes and the wholesale closure of the docks have resulted in a poverty of spirit which will take many years to put right.

I hope residents of what is now the London Borough of Newham, and visitors alike, will enjoy this nostalgic tramride along streets rich in local colour. Our glimpse of the past has been made possible by the following photographers and collectors of tramway views. My special thanks go to: John Price (for the loan of pictures from the late

G.N.Southerden), C.Carter, Alan Cross, R.Elliott, R.W.Kidner, D.W.K.Jones, M.J.O'Connor and John Meredith. My gratitude also to Rosy Thacker and Glynn Wilton of the National Tramway Museum who have both performed miracles of archival excellence to ensure that this book reached a suitable state for publication. Herbert Lingwood was a local resident and his help has been invaluable in preparing this book. The car drawings are the skilled work of Terry Russell who has contributed much to the series. The preparation of some of the photographs has been in the capable hands of Stan Letts. The tickets have kindly been provided by Godfrey Croughton.

Last but not least, my wife Janet and my three children have been very supportive in putting up with my life long passion for tramways.

GEOGRAPHICAL SETTING

East Ham and West Ham are situated on the north bank of the River Thames in an area once belonging to the county of Essex. Until the advent of urban development the landscape was one of water meadows and marshes bordering the river. The Rivers Lea and Roding form a natural boundary to the district which is now almost totally absorbed into Greater London. However, a sizeable area of open space still survives in the form of Wanstead Flats on the northern edge of the two former boroughs. In 1965 both local authorities were amalgamated to form the Borough of Newham.

The Ordnance Survey maps are to the scale of 25" to 1 mile and date from 1914-16.

HISTORICAL BACKGROUND

At the dawn of recorded history in Britain there were a number of isolated, small settlements adjacent to the Roman road from London to Colchester. Where this highway traversed the River Lea, the name Old Ford perpetuates the original crossing point. Barking Abbey was established in 670 and various monastic communities gradually settled in the area. Although jurisdiction was lodged with the county of Essex, the sheriff of Kent once owned land around North Woolwich and this geographical anomaly of detached local authority territory north of the Thames persisted until the formation of the Greater London Council in 1965!

In medieval times the main thoroughfare from Stratford to Bow played an important part in the transporting of grain to the capital; livestock was normally traded at the markets of Stratford. More permanent lines of communication arrived with the Eastern Counties Railway in 1839. In 1846 railway tracks extended from Stratford to the banks of the Thames, and two years later passengers could journey all the way to North Woolwich, there to transfer to a ferry boat for Woolwich proper and the south bank of the river.

Throughout the whole of the latter half of the nineteenth century the communities of East Ham and West Ham grew apace, with speculative building covering the countryside. This economic surge was fueled by cheap transport and new industries; the draining of the marshes and the opening of the new Victoria Dock in 1855 added to the industrial landscape. Street tramway connections between London and the emerging towns of metropolitan Essex were provided by the North Metropolitan Tramways Company, with the first section opening in 1870 from Whitechapel to Bow. In March 1871 passengers could ride from Stratford to Aldgate at the edge of the City of London, for the sum of three old pence. Workmen were carried for a penny less. Stratford Broadway quickly became the centre of operations and various experiments with early forms of mechanical traction, comprising steam, compressed air and battery power, were conducted over the company's lines. A route along Commercial Road from Aldgate to Poplar was opened in 1872. Leytonstone was reached in 1881. The Manor Park to Stratford and Canning Town Station to Plaistow Green

Gate sections followed in 1886.

Shortly before the turn of the century the impetus to convert to electric traction became unstoppable. Municipal pride dictated that the old horse worked tramways had to be replaced by a more modern form of transit, thus in 1901 East Ham had the honour of being the first local authority in the metropolitan area to inaugurate electric tramways. Lines were constructed from the Ilford boundary on the Romford Road through Manor Park and East Ham to the level crossing with the Beckton railway, and from the West Ham boundary at the Boleyn to the bridge over the Roding at Barking. Extensions soon followed to Aldersbrook, along Plashet Grove, and from the Beckton level crossing to a new terminus in Cyprus Place by the Royal Albert Dock.

In 1904 West Ham Corporation entered the field with new electric tracks along the Barking Road and through Plaistow to Stratford. Joint working was instituted with East Ham where the lines met at the Boleyn. The network of local tramways grew very quickly and soon electric cars were crossing West Ham from the Victoria and Albert Docks in the south to Wanstead Flats and the Leyton boundary at Thatched House in the north. In April 1905 East Ham cars reached Ilford Broadway and in the next year joint services operated by Leyton and West Ham cars began between the Bakers Arms and the V&A Docks. In 1909 a through joint service started from Ilford Broadway to Bow Bridge. Meanwhile, construction was going ahead on the other side of the county boundary and the metals of West Ham Corporation were finally connected to those of the London County Council at Bow Bridge. On 11th May 1909 the major trunk route, Ilford to Aldgate, opened with cars of three undertakings sharing the running. At the same time, LCC, West Ham and Leyton cars inaugurated another important East London link northwards from Stratford Broadway to the Bakers Arms with trams working through to Aldgate.

Many improvements to rolling stock and track layout were carried out in the years before the First World War and in 1912 it was finally possible to travel from Barking to Aldgate via Canning Town and Commercial Road. Vehicles plying this route were supplied by no less than four operators: the LCC, West Ham, East Ham and Barking. Most of the LCC tracks within the county of London were not equipped with overhead wires, so cars employed on through services were fitted with conduit collection gear as well as the usual trolley pole. Change pits between the two electrical systems were established at Mile End for services 61 and 63, and at Iron Bridge, Poplar for services 67 and 69.

Tramway services in the area in January 1913 were as follows:

1 Stratford to the Burnell Arms, East Ham.
2 Stratford Broadway to the Boleyn
                     via Upton Park.
3 Canning Town to V&A Docks.
4 Wanstead Flats to V&A Docks.
5 Wanstead Flats to Canning Town
6 Stratford Broadway to Canning Town
7 Bakers Arms to V&A Docks via Stratford.
8 Bakers Arms to V&A Docks via Forest Gate.
9 Greengate to V&A Docks.
10 Stratford Broadway to the Boleyn via Forest
                     Gate.
61 Aldgate to Bakers Arms.
63 Aldgate to Ilford.
67 Aldgate to East Ham Town Hall.
69 Aldgate to Loxford Bridge, Barking.
The East Ham local service from Wanstead Park to Royal Albert Dock was unnumbered.

Barking Council trams withdrew from the through running agreement in May 1914 and service 69 was subsequently withdrawn; service 67 was extended to Barking Broadway as a replacement. During the First World War large numbers of workers vital to the war effort were transported on the local tramways. Only essential repair work was carried out at this period and improvements to cars and track had to wait for the return of peace. In the early 1920s both corporations began an extensive programme of fleet renovation with the aim of replacing worn out trams, targetting those which still retained open tops. The spectre of motor bus competition loomed large, but the trams continued to hold their own, supplying frequent, cheap and reliable transport. However, the notion that there was an alternative to the expense of maintaining the permanent way began to take root. The alternative in question was the embryonic trolleybus. Such a vehicle had already been

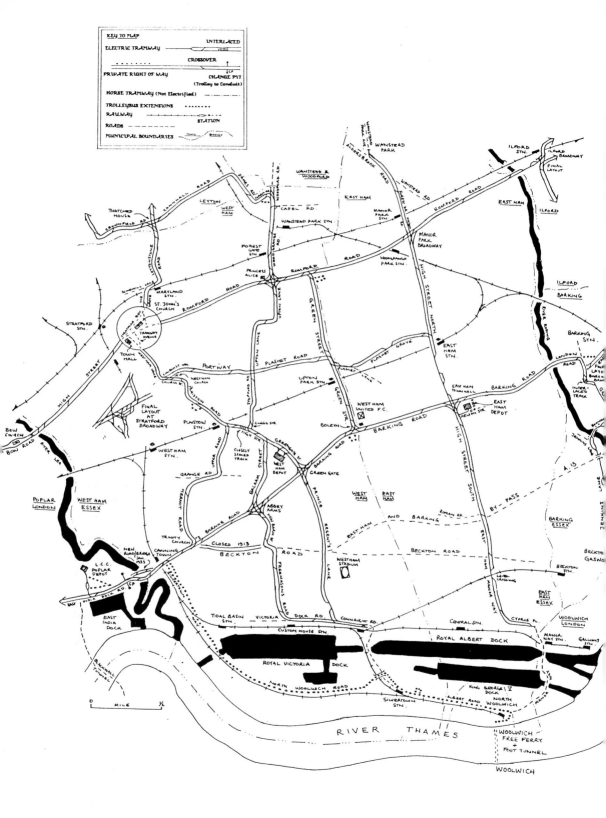

tested by West Ham Corporation in 1912 over some 400 yards of road in Greengate Street, and in 1925 East Ham proposed a trolleybus conversion of the Wanstead Park to RA Docks service. However, the public were having none of it, especially when it emerged that cheap workmen's fares, always associated with tramways, might not be available on the replacing vehicles. The project was quietly shelved and both authorities got on with the task of modernising their tram fleets.

In 1925 West Ham cars ceased to operate on joint service 61; by this time Leyton's tramways had been acquired by the LCC. Further alterations took place in 1926 with West Ham and Walthamstow trams commencing an extended service 7 to Chingford. LCC service 65 was also extended to East Ham Town Hall in peak hours. The years from 1927 to the formation of the London Passenger Transport Board in 1933, saw a stream of new trams appearing. In design they favoured the "tried and tested" LCC standard eight wheel car with enclosed top deck. However, both corporations were enmeshed in a much wider concept of an integrated London wide transport system and all the local tramways were compulsorily acquired by London Transport in 1933. West Ham contributed 134 trams to the new board and East Ham parted with 56. One of the first official acts of the new owners was to close East Ham Depot, which resulted in 20 ex-East Ham bogie cars being transferred to Bow Depot, 23 single truck cars made the short journey to West Ham Depot and any remaining old trams were consigned to Hampstead Depot to await their fate at the hands of the scrapman.

In 1934 the local tram services operated by London Transport were as follows:

1 Stratford to East Ham Town Hall.
1A Stratford to Upton Park, Boleyn.
10 Circular route Stratford Broadway via Forest Gate, Green Street and Plaistow.
61 Leyton, Bakers Arms to Aldgate.
63 Ilford Broadway to Aldgate.
65 East Ham Town Hall to Bloomsbury.
67 Barking to Aldgate.
69 Canning Town to Stratford.
73 RA Docks to Wanstead Park.
87 V&A Docks to Leyton, Bakers Arms.
95 Canning Town to Wanstead Flats.
95A Upton Park, Boleyn to Wanstead Flats.
97 V&A Docks to Chingford.
99 V&A Docks to Stratford.
99A V&A Docks to Greengate.

Two former East Ham cars 21 and 11, now renumbered and repainted in the LT livery of red and cream as cars 53 and 58, were transferred south of the river in 1934 to work service 98 from Abbey Wood Depot. This was the calm before the storm and in 1935 the policy of London Transport to replace most tramways by trolleybuses began to take effect. Scrapping of older four wheel cars started in earnest and in October 1936 service 73 breathed its last, an improved 101 bus route appearing as a replacement. Soon large numbers of LT workmen arrived to erect the new standards and overhead wires need for the replacing trolleybuses. In 1937 trams disappeared from all the local streets save for those still served by the major trunk lines into Aldgate. Service 99A managed to escape until July 1938 when its greyhound racing specials from West Ham Stadium to Plaistow Station fell to the motor bus.

The end of tramways in East London was in sight and the final conversions took place during wartime. Services 61 and 63 went in November 1939 to be followed on 8th June 1940 by services 65 and 67. This final act turned out to be the last trolleybus conversion by London Transport, however, the remaining bogie cars from East and West Ham were spared and redeployed at Abbey Wood Depot where they set to work on services 36, 38, 40, 44 and 46. Former West Ham single truck car 102 was preserved and it now resides at the London Transport Museum in Covent Garden. The fate of its sisters was harsher, and the last former East London cars met a fiery end at Penhall Road scrapyard when London said goodbye to its trams in 1952. Withdrawal of local trolleybus routes began in 1959 and the era of electric street traction finally ended in April 1960 with the closure to trolleybuses of West Ham Depot.

Although the tramways are now but a distant memory, electric rail vehicles, similar to modern single deck tramcars, have returned to the area in the shape of the Docklands Light Railway, the first section of which was opened in August 1987. It was extended past the former docks to terminate at a new development in Beckton in March 1994.

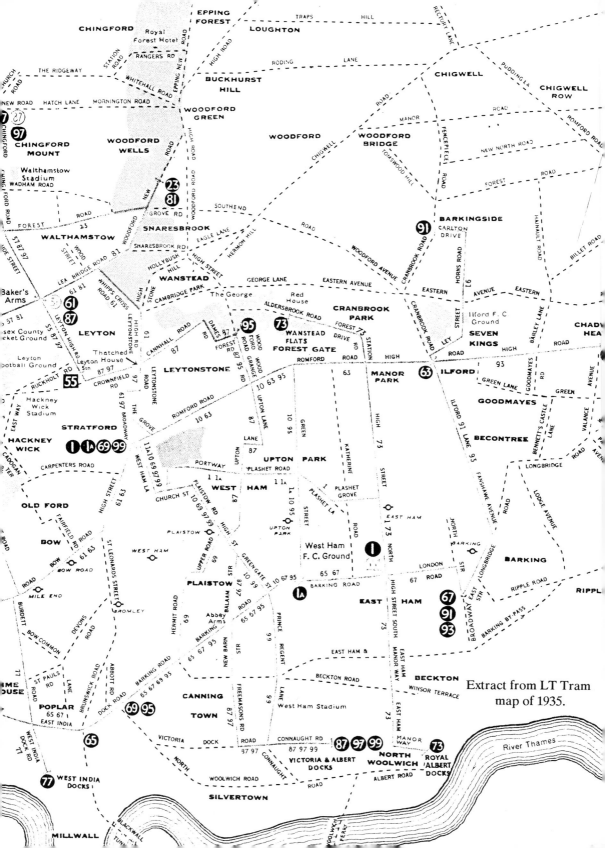

Extract from LT Tram map of 1935.

1. East Ham Tramways
ROYAL ALBERT DOCKS AND BECKTON

1. Cranes and warehouses form the backdrop to car 269 which is standing at the Royal Albert Docks terminus of the former East Ham Corporation Tramways. The date is October 1936 and an official London Transport notice of impending bus replacement is pasted on the rocker panel of the tram. (A.B.Cross)

2. Car 263 now occupies the terminal stub. The main road to North Woolwich veers to the right and a few yards further on it is crossed by the county boundary between Essex and London. Earlier attempts by East Ham to extend the tracks southwards were always thwarted by the presence of several swing bridges which would have delayed the service. Such an extension would also have involved expensive special trackwork and overhead installations. (R.J.Harley Coll.)

3. This 1932 view shows car 50 in full East Ham livery waiting outside the newsagents in Cyprus Place. This area has since been altered by massive road and housing "improvements", which have resulted in new dual carriageways and their associated roundabouts. Visitors to the area can get a glimpse of former times in the splendid North Woolwich Old Station Museum which was opened in 1984. (R.W.Kidner)

4. Shortly after the takeover by LT in 1933, car 13 slows with the end of the track in sight. This car will then reverse for a shortworking to East Ham Town Hall. Along the section from Wanstead Park to RA Docks there were several crossovers which were used for trams not completing the full service. The replacing 101 bus route was also worked in sections. (M.J.O'Connor)

5. The level crossing with the Beckton branch is the scene as a couple of workmen resume their duties after the tram has gone past. The signal box on the right was a Great Eastern Railway model and it controlled the crossing gates and the tramway signal guarding the single track. Behind the tram is a bridge carrying the Gas Light and Coke Company's headshunt line for Beckton Gasworks. Construction started in 1868 on what was to become the largest gasworks in the world; the internal railway system totalled some 75 miles of track serving buildings which covered 360 acres of land. (G.N.Southerden)

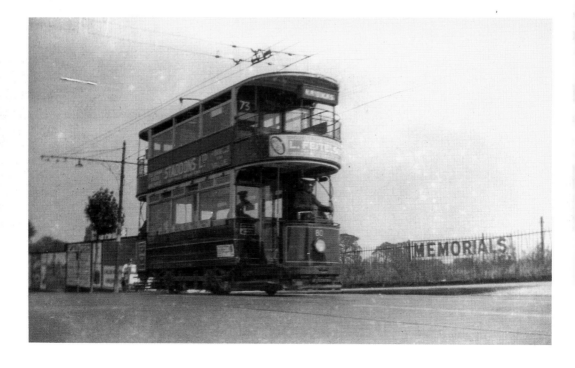

6. Car 7 is still in open top condition as it crosses the Beckton railway. Note the tramway semaphore signal to the right of the tram. The passenger service on the railway outlived the trams by four years and it effectively ended with the bombing of autumn 1940. Both gasworks and railway closed completely in 1971. However, in March 1994 the Docklands Light Railway was extended to a new station quite close to the location of this photograph. (R.J.Harley Coll.)

7. The skate in the overhead above car 80 operates the traffic lights at the junction of High Street South and the A13. Other vehicles activated pads in the road which would be positioned either side of the tram rails. (G.N.Southerden)

8. The motorman of car 72 is about to apply power so that he can use the crossover opposite Roman Road. This was a usual shortworking spot and the tram has already gained several passengers for the return trip to Wanstead Park. (D.W.K.Jones)

EAST HAM DEPOT

9.   This is the official 1901 photo of the electricity works and the car sheds situated in Nelson Street. The depot was further extended and rebuilt in 1909 to cope with the increased fleet needed to operate joint services to London. (Tramway and Railway World)

10.   The original depot measured 148'/45 metres by 65'/20 metres and had a capacity of 25 cars. In this interior view everything is spotless, not even a used ticket sullies the pristine condition of the tracks and the maintenance pits!   (Tramway and Railway World)

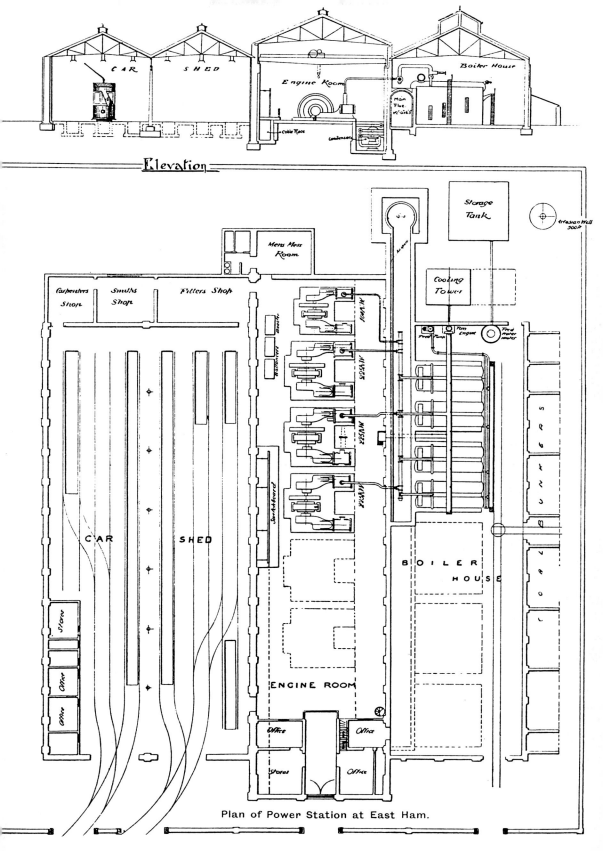

Plan of Power Station at East Ham.

EAST HAM HIGH STREET
AND TOWN CENTRE

11. A service 1 car has just crossed Barking Road in this late 1930s scene outside East Ham Town Hall. A former West Ham bogie car, now in LT livery, waits with a clutch of motor vehicles for the green light, whilst the younger generation is wheeled sedately over the tramlines. (H.Wightman)

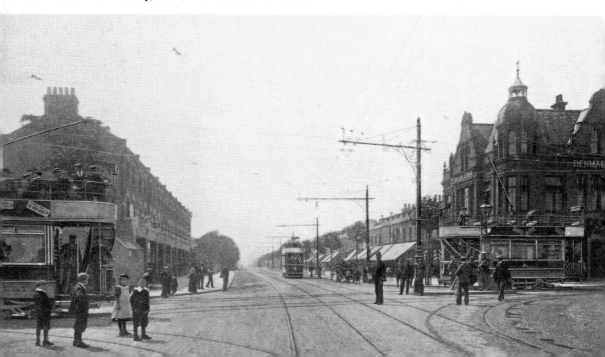

STAR
FURNISHING
CO

DAILY MAIL

12. Excitement is in the air as the latest electric transport wonders parade outside the Denmark Arms. Aside from the trams there is precious little else for the policeman on point duty to control. Many of the tramway junctions were altered later as connecting curves were changed to suit traffic conditions and new services. (Tramway and Railway World)

13. In order to keep the tramways working efficiently the track had to be maintained and renewed on a regular basis. Just such a process is seen here with a standard London County Council car using the Barking Road tracks in the background. Mechanical assistance in the form of the concrete mixer has appeared to alleviate some of the manual chores, but in general the whole task was very labour intensive. Granite setts and woodblocks are piled in the centre by the south to east curve of the junction. (H.Lingwood Coll.)

14. We are now looking east along Barking Road just after the turn of the century. Car 20 could easily outpace the horse drawn traffic as it makes its way towards the West Ham boundary at Green Street. The street lighting of the period was vastly enhanced by the arc lamps of Messrs Johnson and Phillips, several of which can be noted attached to the tramway bracket arms. (J.H.Price Coll.)

529.—SERVICE No. 73—FARES WHEN RUNNING TO AND FROM DEPOT.

Notice to Inspectors and Conductors—West Ham Depot.

The fares to be charged on Service No. 73 when running to and from West Ham Depot are as follows :—

West Ham Depot, and

Green Street	1d.
East Ham Town Hall	1½d.
East Ham Station or Charlemont Road	2d.
Ruskin Avenue or Beckton Road	2½d.
Manor Park Station or R.A. Docks	3d.
Wanstead Park	3½d.

Greengate Street (Barking Road), and

East Ham Town Hall	1d.
East Ham Station or Charlemont Road	1½d.
Ruskin Avenue or Beckton Road	2d.
Manor Park Station or R.A. Docks	2½d.
Wanstead Park	3d.

Green Street (Boleyn), and

East Ham Station or Charlemont Road	1d.
Ruskin Avenue or Beckton Road	1½d.
Manor Park Station or R.A. Docks	2d.
Wanstead Park	2½d.

Return tickets (ordinary or workmen) must not be issued for these journeys.

15. After East Ham Depot closed in 1933, cars operating service 73 were shedded at West Ham which required an off route journey along Barking Road. Car 279 with "Beckton Road" on the indicator blind is on one of these depot runs. (J.H.Meredith Coll.)

16. There is still a rural feel to Plashet Grove as car 1 rumbles towards Upton Park. On construction of the tramway it was stipulated that the trees had to be protected. The carriageway was raised so as not to disturb the tree roots and single track was deemed appropriate so that the overhead wires could be placed away from the branches. Needless to say, subsequent highway "planners" had different ideas and this scene has now vanished for good. (R.J.Harley Coll.)

17. At the end of Plashet Lane by the Duke of Edinburgh public house, we witness the meeting of the two corporations, for this is the boundary separating East Ham from its western neighbour. The tracks of the two authorities were connected at this point in November 1907. East Ham covered top car 39 is actually in Green Street and is about to make the turn to the driver's left. A West Ham open top car waits to enter the single track. (J.H.Price Coll.)

MANOR PARK

18. We now reach Manor Park Broadway at the junction with Romford Road. Car 17 was delivered in July 1901 and was fitted with a top cover in 1908. Here it seems to have been hired by a private party and consequently it displays SPECIAL CAR on the front indicator blind. (R.J.Harley Coll.)

19. The view on the opposite side of the road also features car 17. Note the complete lack of any other motorised vehicles at this time. (R.J.Harley Coll.)

20. Romford Road, Manor Park and West Ham car 108 halts for the photographer. Above the trolley pole can be seen the bracket arm with the heavier feed wires which supplied the overhead with electric current. (R.J.Harley Coll.)

WANSTEAD PARK

21. The terminus known as Wanstead Park could more accurately be described as Aldersbrook; the end of the track was at the intersection of Aldersbrook Road and Wanstead Park Avenue. Car 24 is pictured in 1927. (G.N.Southerden)

22. Geoffrey Southerden, the photographer, has now positioned himself behind car 24 as it prepares to leave on the 48 minute run to the Royal Abert Docks. Fortunately another tram will be along in about four minutes, such was the service in those days! Note the abandoned stretch of track in the foreground. (G.N.Southerden)

No. 257.—WANSTEAD PARK TERMINUS.

NOTICE TO STAFF—WEST HAM DEPOT.

The staff are notified that at the above terminus all passengers must alight at the motorman's end of car.

23. Hazy sunshine greets the next arrival, car 41, which has been equipped earlier in its life with conduit pick up gear to enable it to work through services over LCC tracks. However, it has now been relegated to purely local duties and it will be scrapped in 1933. (G.N.Southerden)

24. Car 211 is framed by the ponds and trees of Wanstead Flats on 17th October 1936 . It is waiting to leave on one of the last service 73 journeys. Unusually for East London this section was not converted to trolleybuses. (J.H.Meredith Coll.)

JOINT SERVICES

25. The short distance along Ilford Hill to the Broadway was ceded very early on by Ilford Corporation to the through service operated by East Ham, West Ham and LCC trams. Former East Ham car 59 now repainted as LT car 89, waits at the terminus of service 63 in June 1938. The Ilford and Barking tramways will feature in a later Middleton Press album. (W.A.Camwell)

26. East Ham cars also reached Stratford Broadway. In the summer of 1933 car 16 has just been acquired by the recently formed London Passenger Transport Board and sports the suffix letter C after the fleet number. The municipal coat of arms has already been removed from the waist panel of the tram. (G.N.Southerden)

27. The motorman has left his post as car 95 is stranded on a bleak Barking Road. The tram has had its fenders painted white and its headlamp masked to conform with wartime blackout regulations. Trolleybus fittings have already been erected for the next generation of electric traction vehicles. (Lens of Sutton)

28. Broadside on, the East Ham trams with their domed roofs were trim and neat four wheel cars. The smart, clean appearance is also noteworthy; the letters EAST HAM TRAMWAYS were gold shaded blue. This tram waits at Barking for the 46 minute journey on service 67 to Aldgate. The return fare was nine old pence and cars ran every two to four minutes. (G.N.Southerden)

EAST HAM ROLLING STOCK

Both undertakings described in this book were active in rebuilding older vehicles, this sometimes resulted in renumbering of trams, occasionally newer vehicles took the fleet numbers of cars which had already been scrapped. When London Transport took over, the remaining East Ham and West Ham trams were again renumbered. It is beyond the scope of this book to go into great detail of all the movements of rolling stock and the reader should consult "The Tramways of East London" by Rodinglea, published in 1967, and "Tramways in Metropolitan Essex" (vol 2) by V.E.Burrows, published in 1976, for further information.

Cars 1 - 35. These were traditional, four wheel, open top cars with reversed stairs; they rode on Brill 21E trucks of 6ft wheelbase. Cars 1 - 15 were supplied in March 1901 from the Electric Railway and Tramway Carriage Works at Preston. The last five cars of the 1 - 35 batch reached East Ham in 1903. Apart from cars 1, 2, 4 and 7 all the rest were top covered and some were converted with longer wheelbase trucks and conduit gear for the joint services to London. Nine cars survived to be renumbered and repainted in LT livery. The final few cars were scrapped in 1935.

Cars 36 - 40. These were basically similar to the previous batch, except that they were delivered in 1905 as covered top cars.

Cars 41 - 45. Delivered in 1910, these trams had direct stairs and were fitted with 7ft 6ins wheelbase trucks equipped with conduit gear.

Car 46. Formerly Barking Council car 9, this tram passed to East Ham in 1915. It was a

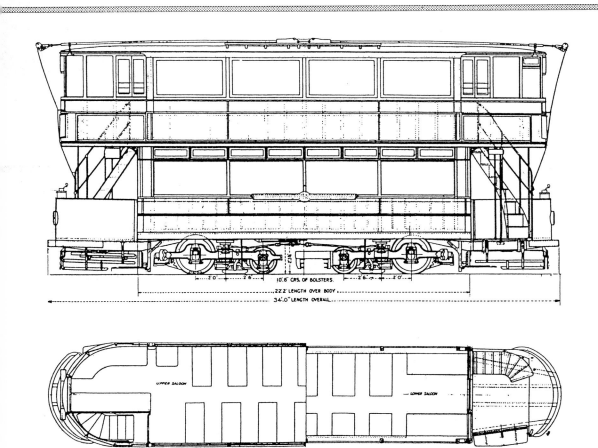

standard three window, covered top four wheel car originally fitted with conduit gear.

Cars 47-52, 37-40. Built by the Brush Company at Loughborough in 1921, these were covered top, single truck cars. Each tram had open balconies and a flat roof. The whole batch survived into LT days and they were scrapped in 1935.

Cars 51 - 70. The pride of the fleet, these eight wheel cars were delivered from Brush in 1927/8 and were placed in service on the major trunk services to London. In 1933, much to the chagrin of some local enthusiasts, the new owners removed the whole batch to Bow Depot, where they performed mainly on service 63. They were later fitted with windscreens by London Transport, and after the local services were replaced by trolleybuses, they were transferred south of the river to Abbey Wood Depot. Here they worked out their days on services 36, 38, 44 and 46 until 5th July 1952 when tramway operation in the capital ceased.

The livery of East Ham Corporation Tramways has variously been described as a rich, reddish brown and yellowish cream, or a coffee coloured brown and cream. The borough coat of arms appeared on the waist panel and underneath, on the rocker panel, the name of the undertaking was picked out in gold letters, shaded blue.

29. East Ham car 30 is being towed by an E/1 ex-LCC car at Manor House on 25th August 1933. The car was being taken for a repaint in LT livery and it subsequently reappeared as no. 61. (M.J.O'Connor)

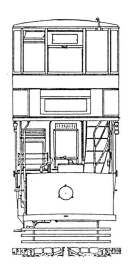

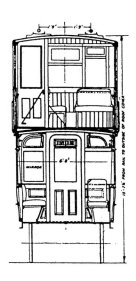

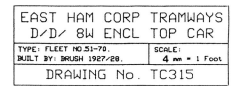

EAST HAM CORP TRAMWAYS
D/D/ 8W ENCL TOP CAR

| TYPE: FLEET NO.51-70. | SCALE: |
| BUILT BY: BRUSH 1927/28. | 4 mm = 1 Foot |

DRAWING No. TC315

SCALE FEET   0 1 2 3 4 5 6 7 8 9 10 11 12

30. This is ex-East Ham car 15, but in full LT red and cream livery and renumbered 49. Note that it retains the outmoded reversed stairs which limited the motorman's field of vision. (D.W.K.Jones)

32. LT car 97, a former East Ham bogie car, is seen in London Transport Livery in the late 1930s. (C.Carter)

31. Beautifully turned out, car 56 is seen at Stratford. As delivered these trams had the plough carrier fixed to one of the trucks, these were removed later and centrally mounted carriers were fitted by Charlton Works in 1941. (K.H.Rudolph)

33. Car 97 makes a reappearance this time equipped with driver's windscreens. This 1952 view at Eltham shows the final condition of these trams, which had given such sterling service to the people of London. (C.Carter)

34. The top deck interior of car 87 is plain and severely functional. The seat under the front number indicator box was a favourite with younger passengers. (J.C.Gillham)

2. West Ham Tramways

VICTORIA AND ALBERT
DOCKS

35. At the end of the line in Connaught Road, car 224 is poised for the return to Stratford Broadway on service 99. In the October 1934 LT service renumbering scheme, the original West Ham service 9 had the extra digit added. In June 1937, when the trolleybuses arrived, the route number was expanded to 699. (D.W.K.Jones)

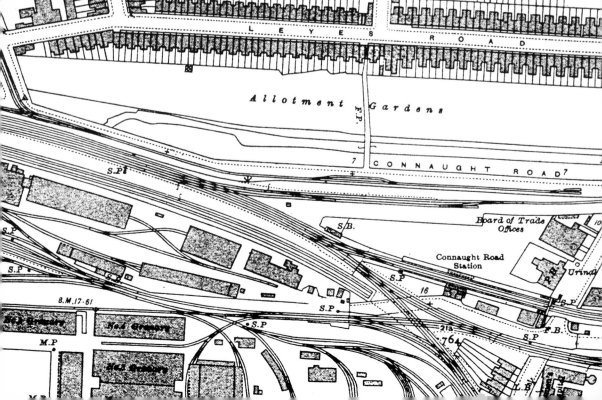

36. Behind the two trams the level crossing gate of the Beckton branch can be glimpsed and to the right of car 1721 is the old Great Western Railway goods depot. The Victoria Dock was the first in the world to have a purpose built railway system. Both trams are on service 97 to Chingford Mount, an hour's journey away. (D.W.K.Jones)

37. The scissors crossover at the Docks terminus was ideal for the many car movements needed to cope with heavy passenger loadings of dock workers. (G.N.Southerden)

38. Four members of the original West Ham fleet come together at the Abbey Arms junction in 1905. As is usual in these early photos, great public interest attended the arrival of the man with the camera! (H.Lingwood Coll.)

39. Shortly after the formation of London Transport, car 134 halts at Canning Town in August 1933. (M.J.O'Connor)

40. Service 95 was replaced by trolleybuses in September 1937, and in the last week of tramway operation car 226 reverses on the Canning Town crossover opposite the Westminster Bank. (H.Lingwood Coll.)

WALTHAMSTOW AND WEST HAM DEPOTS.

CONVERSION TO TROLLEYBUS—WEST HAM AREA.

On Sunday, 12th September, 1937, tram routes 1, 1a and 95 will be converted to trolleybus operation as shewn.

Tram Routes 1 and 1a will operate as a circular trolleybus Route 689, via :—Stratford Broadway, Portway, Green Street, Barking Road, High Street North, Plashet Grove, Plashet Road, Portway, Stratford Broadway, and in the reverse direction.

Tram Route 95 will be converted to trolleybus between Canning Town Station and Wanstead Flats, and will be extended via Crownfield Road, High Road Leyton, Grange Park Road and Church Road, to join up with trolleybus Route 685, now operating between Walthamstow ("Crooked Billet") and Lea Bridge Road. The through route Walthamstow ("Crooked Billet") and Canning Town Station will be numbered 685.

Specimens of revised tickets and farebills are exhibited in West Ham Depot, and must be closely studied for new fares.

41. At Iron Bridge, Canning Town a new road was opened in January 1933. The tram tracks were realigned and a new change pit installed. In the background the face of well known London politician, Herbert Morrison, lends weight to the election campaign as car 334 prepares to depart from the change pit. (D.W.K.Jones)

42. Into the LCC area, and we enter the Metropolitan Borough of Poplar. Opposite Leamouth Road the overhead wires begin and the tram shown here will shortly shoot its plough at the adjacent change pit. (K.H.Rudolph)

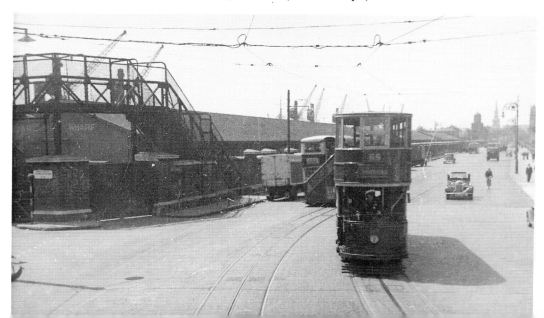

43. We leave service 67 at the East India Dock Tavern by the northern entrance to the Blackwall Tunnel. The East India Docks with the imposing entrance gateway were constructed in 1805/6 and a century later the boundary wall by East India Dock Road had to be set back to allow construction of the LCC electric tramway. (R.J.Harley Coll.)

44. On our return to West Ham territory, we encounter car 327 at the Green Gate junction. From the look of the overhead it would seem that all the back street tram routes have already been converted to trolleybuses. As this was near the depot, crew changes were common here and passengers had to wait a short time for a replacement motorman and conductor. (H.B.Priestley)

45. Car 291 stands at the terminus in Green Street outside the Boleyn. In the background a former LCC M class car proceeds along Barking Road. When football specials were needed for the nearby West Ham United ground at Upton Park, the duty inspector would phone up the depot and a line of empty trams would duly appear. Such was the efficiency of the system that vast crowds could be shifted quickly with the minimum of fuss. (H.Wightman)

UPTON AND PLAISTOW

46. A tram is pictured opposite the Carlton Cinema in Green Street. In the distance is the Forest Gate bus garage which was closed by London Transport in April 1960.
(J.H.Price Coll.)

47. High Street, Plaistow at the junction with Clegg Street and a tram on service 7A waits for the right of way to be indicated by the signal on the traction standard. In this narrow street the rails of the double track were so close together that trams were unable to pass one another. At peak times this was a considerable bottle neck especially when the automatic points leading to Clegg Street failed. Many a motorman was subjected to a blast of good natured East London banter from the dockers leaning over the balcony on the top deck, when he had to reverse the car and use a point iron to gain the correct track. (G.N.Southerden)

1470.—NOTICE—SIGNALS, HIGH STREET, PLAISTOW.

The attention of Drivers is drawn to the signals controlling the narrow part of High Street, Plaistow, near Clegg Street.

Signal lights are fixed on—

Pole No. 140	to	Stratford
Pole No. 141	to	Docks

and after passing under the operating skates Drivers must not proceed through the narrow way until they receive the green signal.

No tram or trolleybus must be run under the operating skate or follow another vehicle through until the preceding vehicle has cleared the line.

814.—ELECTRICALLY OPERATED POINTS AND FROGS.

Notice to Motormen.

New type operating mechanism is being installed at :—

Plaistow Hill, Upper Road junction.

Forest Road, Woodford New Road junction.

The first skate controls the electrically operated frog and selects the wire which the trolley will take. For the *straight* road cars must pass under with power *off*; for the *branch* road cars must pass under with power *on*.

The second skate controls the track points and operates independently of any action by the driver. Cars can pass under with power on or off.

A signal will indicate to the driver which road his car will take, thus :—

Track set for
Straight.   Track set for
                                                  Branch.

Motormen are specially instructed that they must take power or coast under the first skate according to which road they wish to take. It is not sufficient to coast if the points are already set for the branch road—the car must pass under with power on.

48. The first car in Plaistow was an altogether more genteel affair with the mayor and corporation presenting the new transport system to the populus. (J.H.Meredith Coll.)

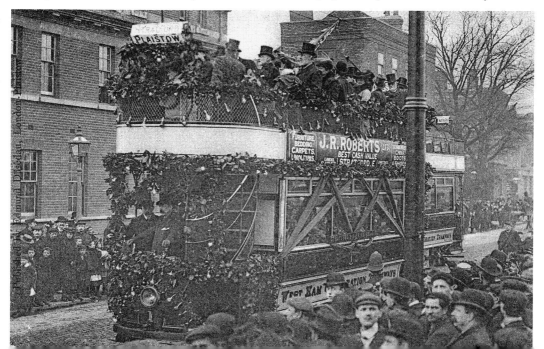

49. Although there are no appreciable gradients in this part of the world, the West Ham trams had to cope with many narrow streets and sharp bends. Here is the scene at the junction of Terrace Road and Stopford Road. Where there was little room between the tramrails and the kerb, routine deliveries made by the coalman took on an element of farce as the horse and sack laden cart had to meander back and forth dodging the tramcars. (J.H.Price Coll.)

50. The tram service had just been opened when this postcard was produced of the crossroads with Portway, Plashet Road, Upton Lane and Stopford Road. (J.H.Meredith Coll.)

51. In Upton Lane by the Spotted Dog, car 34 bites into the curve on its way to Wanstead Flats. Note the rotary destination indicator. (W.Hornby)

52. Car 275 is already using the positive wire of the new trolleybus overhead in West Ham Lane. Soon this route will be served exclusively by the newer vehicles, however, the granite setted roadway will endure and actually outlive the trolleybuses! (C.Carter)

53. We now take the opportunity to board car 1348 heading for Stratford Broadway, one of the most important London tramway junctions and a mecca for enthusiasts. (A.B.Cross)

STRATFORD

54. Right up to the late 1930s you could stand at Stratford Broadway, if you were so minded, and watch the trams for hours. On the south eastern approach to the junction, in the appropriately named Tramway Avenue, a brace of trams can be seen waiting for the return journey. Often cars in peak hours would terminate before the Broadway due to the sheer volume of tramway traffic occupying every inch of available track. (C.Carter)

55. Car 276 stands at the top of Tramway Avenue; it will shortly reverse and set off in the direction of East Ham. (C.Carter)

56. St.John's Church occupies the centre of Stratford Broadway and just in front of the churchyard we meet up again with car 1348 working service 97EX. In the foreground the driver of car 293 notches up on his controller as he negotiates the sharp bend away from the terminal stand. (A.B.Cross)

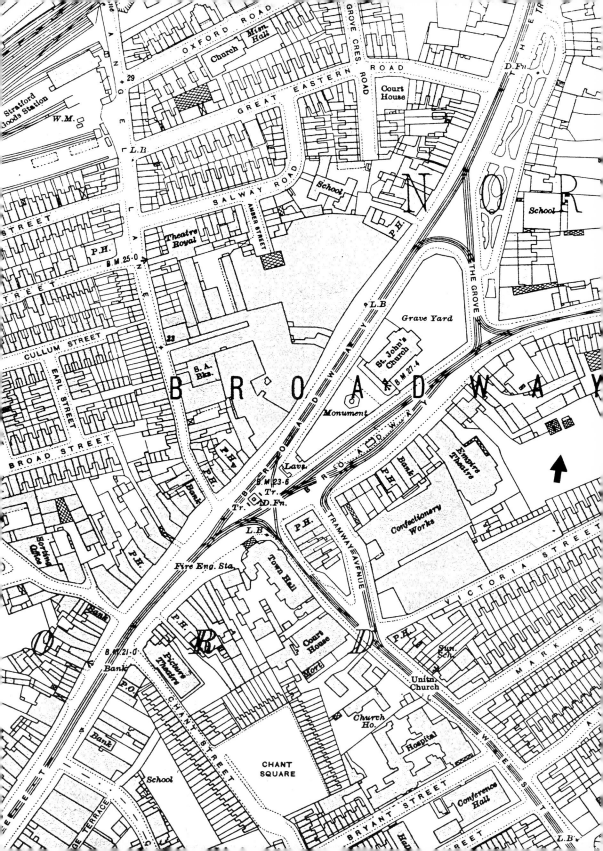

57. Looking west towards the Town Hall, we catch sight of car 1435 on service 97. A picture of this tram in original LCC condition is included in companion Tramway Classics volume *Greenwich and Dartford Tramways*. The two young ladies in straw hats are modelling the latest in 1936 fashions. (H.Wightman)

58. A passenger shelter was provided by the corporation and was used to advertise the benefits of domestic electricity. At night it was illuminated. (C.Carter)

59. On the south side of the shelter the crew
dressed in their white topped summer caps
pose for the photographer. (A.B.Cross)

60. Lunchtime at Stratford and West Ham car 89, seemingly devoid of humanity, waits for the crew to turn up after they have managed a quick sandwich. (G.N.Southerden)

61. The main line service to Aldgate passed the other side of the loading island. Here passengers could change to the purely local back street routes leading southwards to Plaistow and the docks, and eastwards to East Ham and Beckton. Car 2061, seen here, was once part of the Walthamstow Corporation fleet. (C.Carter)

62. Following the Walthamstow theme, we next meet a four wheel car from that fleet. Here car 2016, in LT red and cream livery, shows service 7 on its number blind. Car 216 adjacent does not have this facility and has to make do with a number 1 disc placed over the headlamp. (A.B.Cross)

63. Summertime and even though the local streets were not noted for their scenic qualities, the open balconies of these two trams look inviting for a pleasant excursion. (R.J.Harley Coll.)

64. Trams galore! Some idea of the intensity of service can be gained from this picture. The top deck windows have been wound down by the conductor in response to the warm weather, but the motorman of car 267 is still expected to wear full uniform and to look smart at all times. (A.B.Cross)

65. We now step out into the main road quite safely as there are few private motorists to delay our walk across to one of the newer West Ham eight wheel cars employed on the Aldgate to Ilford service. (G.N.Southerden)

No. 220.—WHITE CAP COVERS AND WHITE COATS.

THE STAFF ARE REMINDED THAT WHITE CAP COVERS MUST BE WORN CONTINUOUSLY FROM MAY 1st TO SEPTEMBER 30th.

WHITE COATS (TROLLEY BUS DRIVERS) MUST BE WORN FROM JUNE 1st TO SEPTEMBER 30th, AND MAY BE WORN IN MAY.

No. 221.—CARE OF UNIFORM.

Employees' attention is called to the following information for the purpose of keeping their uniforms smart and in good condition :—

Chromium Buttons.—Buttons can be kept clean by being briskly rubbed with a wash-leather. They must not be cleaned with polish.

White Sleeve Bands.—A daily sponging will keep the bands clean and remove dirt, which should not be allowed to work into the texture, causing discoloration.

Rexine Piping.—Rexine piping should be cleaned with a damp cloth. Care should be taken to ensure that the cloth is only damp, not wet, and to avoid rubbing the material of the uniform.

Flapless Pockets.—To preserve the shape and appearance of the uniform care should be taken to avoid excessive loading of the pockets.

Brushing.—To brush the uniform daily is more effective than a weekly clean up. Dust is more easily removed and damage to the material prevented.

66. The spire of St.John's Church constructed in 1834, forms the background to car 310. The motorman seems to be perturbed by something going on upstairs. (A.B.Cross)

67. A tram freshly painted in London Transport livery still lacks the familiar LT gold fleet name on the waist panel. On the other side of the Broadway, you could purchase a bargain piano ideal for those family get togethers in an age before television killed off traditional home entertainment. (G.N.Southerden)

68. The conductor of car 99 points out something to a passenger as he sweeps past a clutter of street furniture which includes a red phone box, a tram stop attached to a green painted traction standard and the entrance sign to a public convenience. (H.B.Priestley)

69. Taken in the infancy of the system, this portrait of the tram terminus reveals the measured pace of life in Edwardian times. This view is postmarked September 1907. (J.H.Price Coll.)

Notice to Motormen and Conductors.

As from the first car on Monday, 17th December, 1934, inward bound cars on Service No. 61 will work via " The Grove " and stop to pick up and set down passengers at the island in The Broadway (south side) east of Tramway Avenue.

The points at the junction of " The Grove " and The Broadway (north side) will be set for cars to turn into " The Grove."

After leaving the stopping place in The Broadway, cars will not stop again for passengers until reaching the stopping place at Chant Street, High Street.

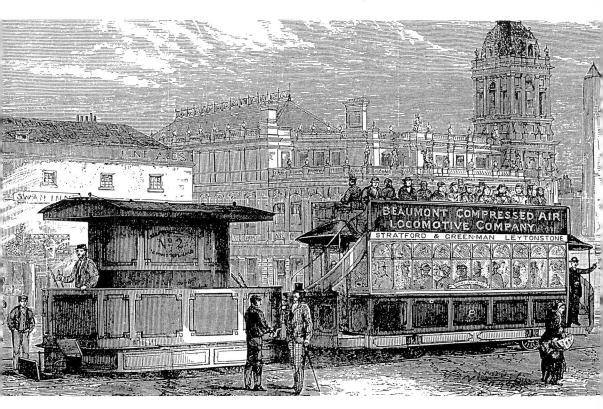

70. Car 45 is on a trial run in 1905 as it joins the tracks in Romford Road. The tram is surrounded by curious bystanders, and for many of those watching, this new form of transport will mean that, for the first time, trips out towards the countryside are possible. Cheap workmen's fares would also add to the mobility of the labour force and the "missus" could travel to the shops for a wider variety of goods. (Tramway Museum Society)

71. An earlier visitor to Stratford was this contraption. Seen by its inventor, Colonel F.E.B.Beaumont, as the answer to the tramway company's prayers in speeding up the horse car service, the compressed air tramcar of 1881 makes its debut. The leading vehicle is taking on air through a flexible hose connection from a tank situated under the road. The service between Leytonstone and Stratford ran for a short time, but without much success, so the faithful horse was reinstated. The system was used effectively in France subsequently. (Illustrated London News)

72. The Town Hall, which was opened in July 1869, was described as "a handsome stone-fronted building in the Italian Renaissance style, with a lofty tower." Another object of beauty, in its crimson lake and primrose colours, is LCC car 1349, outbound to Aldgate. (J.H.Price Coll.)

73. On the London side of the Broadway there is plenty of public transport about in this mid 1930s scene. (H.Wightman)

74. Samuel Gurney was a Quaker philanthropist and banker who died in 1856. At his memorial obelisk on the western side of the Broadway, the tram services from Ilford and Leyton joined company for the run down the High Street to Bow Bridge. (C.Carter Coll.)

75. Late in the reign of Queen Victoria, all traffic in this view is horse drawn. The horse car service first opened in March 1871 and it was soon extended to Leytonstone; trams on the Aldgate to Leytonstone line were painted blue, and the through journey took just over the hour at a very leisurely pace. (J.H.Price Coll.)

76. Around 1890 two horse trams are captured on film outside the Swan Hotel, Stratford. The depot track curves behind the trams and this can be located on the accompanying plan of Stratford Broadway. (J.H.Price Coll.)

77. The Grove leads out of Stratford towards Maryland Point and Leytonstone. Shortly before the electrification of these tracks, we witness the rare sight of a horse tram being passed by a horseless carriage. This was the dawn of the motor age in West Ham. (J.H.Price Coll.)

78. At Maryland Point the Stratford to Leytonstone horse car plods its weary way. Note the local pride evident in this postcard with the West Ham coat of arms embossed above the tram. (J.H.Price Coll.)

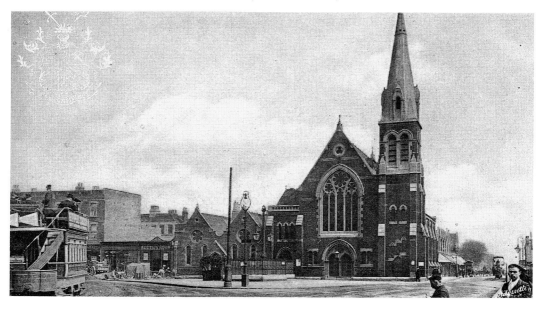

Horse tramway layout at Stratford Broadway taken
from the 1895 edition of the 1:1056 OS map.

79. In June 1937 car 232 turns into Crownfield Road at the Thatched House junction. An E3 type car on service 61 passes in the background. Very soon service 97 will pass into history and no more will the clatter of four wheel trams crossing the points be heard. Instead residents will have to accustom themselves to the almost unnatural quietness of the replacing trolleybuses. (A.B.Cross)

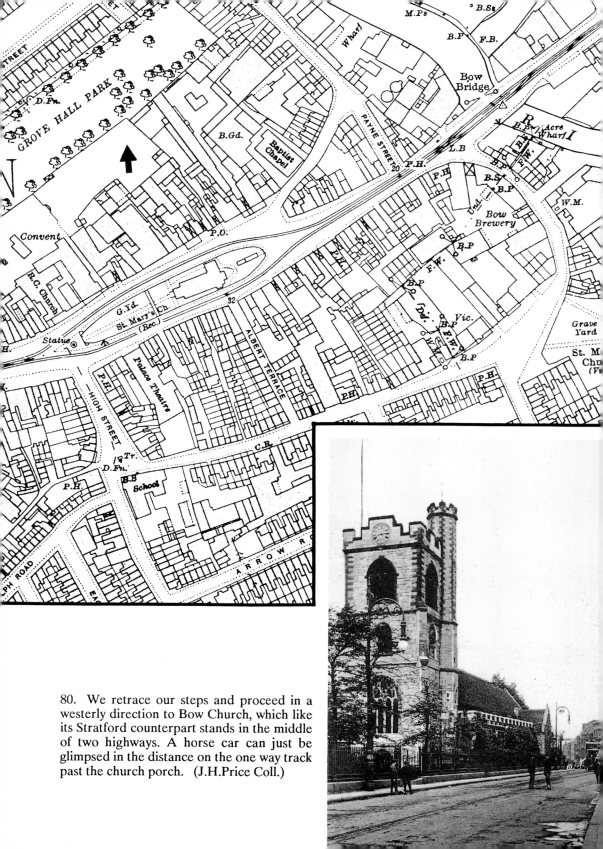

80. We retrace our steps and proceed in a westerly direction to Bow Church, which like its Stratford counterpart stands in the middle of two highways. A horse car can just be glimpsed in the distance on the one way track past the church porch. (J.H.Price Coll.)

81. Service 63 encountered LCC conduit tracks at the change pit outside Mile End Station. The driver of former East Ham car 52 waits patiently for the plough to be inserted under his car, then he will move forward and finally the conductor will lower and stow the trolley pole. (J.H. Price Coll.)

Ni 5919

70B London Passenger
Transport Board Tramway

6d Work

Bakers Arms
and
Aldgate

Bakers Arms
and
Bow Road Stn (B.R.)

61 & 63
Green Man
and
Aldgate

Ilford Broadway
and
Aldgate

Green Street
(Romford Road)
and Aldgate

Ticket issued subject to by-laws and regulations of the Board, must be given up on demand, and only available for a return journey on day of issue. Ni transferable.

VS 8570

[70 P] L.P.T.B. (Tram)

5	Aldgate		Rising Sun	15
6	New Road	61	Bakers Arms	15
7	Stepney Station	63	Whipps Cross or Ilford Bdwy.	14
8	Burdett Road	EX	Forest Glade or Little Ilford Rd	13
9	Blackwall Tunnel	67	Green Man or Manor Pk Bdy	1
10	Canning Town Stn		Leytonstone Station or Katherine Rd	11
11	Abbey Arms, Balaam Street			
1	Aldgate		Green Street, Romford Rd.	
2	Lond. Hosp (Cent.G'ten) or Burdett Rd (East India Dock Road)		Thatch'd House or Woodgrange Road	10
3	Stepney Grn. Stn or Burdett Rd Stn		Maryland Point Stn or Hamfrith Rd.	9
4	Burdett Road (Mile End Rd)	1d & 1½d Ord.	Stratford Broadway	8
5	Bow Road Station		Warton Road	7
Fairfield Rd. (Bow Road)			Bow Bridge	6

FOREST GATE

82. Inspite of appearances it isn't raining on the Romford Road at the turn of the century when this view was taken. The ladies on the top deck are shielding their delicate complexions from the rays of the sun. (C.Carter Coll.)

83. A brewery dray is supplying the Princess Alice Hotel as a horse car on the Manor Park to Stratford service passes by. (J.H.Price Coll.)

84. The electric layout at the Princess Alice once featured a grand union junction so beloved of enthusiasts, however, by the time of this photo the connecting curves from Romford Road (west) to Woodgrange Road, and from Romford Road (west) to Upton Lane had been removed. Car 89 appears sparkling in its LT livery from its new home at Bow Depot. (Lens of Sutton)

85. Car 43 crosses Romford Road just after the service opened in July 1904. (J.H.Meredith Coll.)

86. Woodgrange Road, Forest Gate by the Pricess Alice Hotel and car 80 is about to swing across into Upton Lane on its journey through Plaistow to the V&A Docks. (J.H.Price Coll.)

87. In August 1905 a trade magazine, the Tramway and Railway World, printed an article on the Turner automatic point controller. This picture of the corner of Romford Road (east) and Woodgrange Road was used to illustrate the account. Part of the point controller mechanism is contained in the metal box on the left of the picture. (Tramway and Railway World)

88. From a vantage point above Woodgrange Road, a service car passes below and we catch a rare glimpse of West Ham water car 1A which has escaped the confines of Greengate Street Depot and is out on patrol in the northern half of the borough. It seems to be taking a rest from its duties as the lorry behind tries to overtake. (J.H.Meredith Coll.)

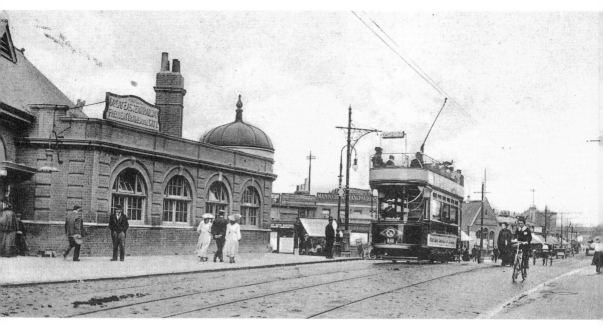

89. Many suburban railway stations such as Forest Gate suffered severe competition when the tramways were electrified. Some railway companies grasped the new technology and the District Railway's electric trains reached East Ham in 1905. Forest Gate had to wait until 1949 for an electric service. (J.H.Price Coll.)

90. In 1921 the Leyton tramways, which had got into a rather parlous state, were taken over by the LCC who then effected much needed improvements to rolling stock and track. Leyton car 52, seen here at Forest Road, Wanstead Flats, has acquired the letters LCC on the waist panel. (G.N.Southerden)

91. Leyton car 15 is at the same spot as the previous photo, only we are now looking towards Wanstead Flats and the junction with Woodford Road. The date is 1927. (G.N.Southerden)

92. The crew of this West Ham tram take a
break at Wanstead Flats terminus. Rather
neatly the line ended where the housing
stopped at the borough boundary.
(G.N.Southerden)

360.—CHILDREN'S HOLIDAY FARES—EAST AND WEST HAM AREAS.

Notice to Inspectors and Conductors—West Ham Depot.

During the period Thursday, 26th July, to Saturday, 25th August (both dates included), *but Sundays and August Bank Holiday excepted*, the following special children's fares will be in operation :—

Fare.	Service.	Journey.
1d. Return	5	Wanstead Flats (Forest Road)—Boleyn.
,,	10	Princess Alice—Boleyn (via Green Street).
,,	8	Wanstead Flats (Forest Road)—Plaistow Broadway.
,,	East Ham	Wanstead Park—East Ham Town Hall.
2d. Return	5	Wanstead Flats (Forest Road)—Canning Town Fire Station.
,,	10	Princess Alice—Greengate.
,,	8	Wanstead Flats (Forest Road)—Docks (Connaught Road).
,,	East Ham	Wanstead Park—Albert Docks.

Specimen tickets will be exhibited in the depot and must be punched on issue in the fare stage point to which available and on the return journey *cancelled* in the fare stage point to which available.

There is no time restriction on the availability of these tickets.

93. Car 65 has reached the terminus in Woodford Road and the conductor is about to swing the trolley pole for the return trip. On fine days the trams would be packed with town dwellers seeking the fresh air and open spaces of the Flats. With this extra traffic in mind, the corporation took the opportunity to lay short lengths of track in Capel Road and Forest Road. The rails in Forest Road were later joined to the Leyton system and the terminal stub in Capel Road was abandoned around 1907. (C.Carter Coll.)

WEST HAM DEPOT

94. When the electric tramways first opened, a temporary depot was constructed on the west side of West Ham Lane. The permanent car sheds illustrated here were completed in 1906.

The site at Greengate Street had a capacity of 150 trams. The building has had a chequered career and has housed trolleybuses and later diesel buses. (Tramway and Railway World)

95. The interior of the unfinished depot clearly shows the maintenance pits which were used by fitters to inspect the trucks and electrical gear of the trams. (Tramway and Railway World)

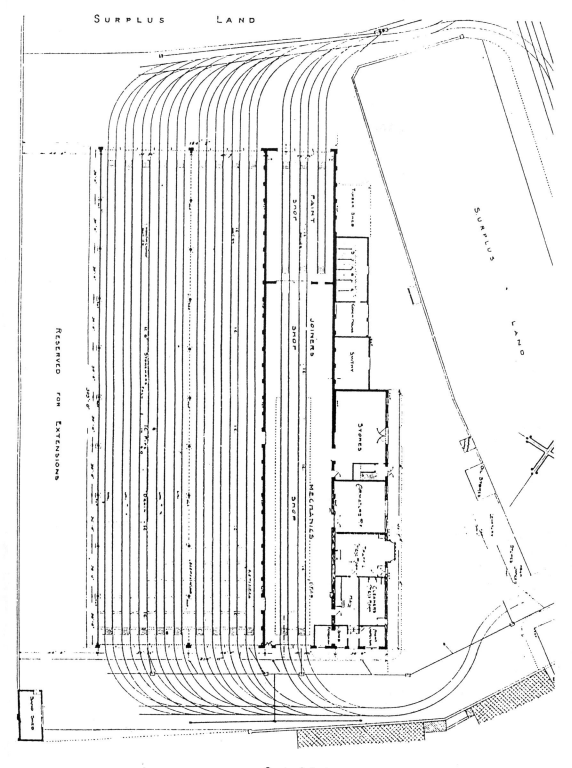

SURPLUS LAND

SURPLUS LAND

RESERVED FOR EXTENSIONS

Scale of Feet

10 5 0   10 20 30 40 50 60 70 80 90 100   150   200

96. There were extensive workshop facilities attached to the depot where, as depicted in this 1912 view, carpenters could assemble new top deck covers. Standing in the bays at the back are two trams awaiting the attention of the paint shop staff. (Tramway and Railway World)

97. Car rebuilding work continued at the depot into the London Transport era. Even though the life expectancy of these trams was limited, they still received much care and attention from this group of craftsmen. (R.Elliott)

WEST HAM ROLLING STOCK

As already mentioned in the East Ham section, this rolling stock list can only give an overview of the West Ham fleet. The corporation became aware that London operating conditions were extremely arduous and from 1921 they began began an extensive programme of designing their own rolling stock and rebuilding existing cars to much tougher specifications. Steel underframes and bodywork strengthening were applied to the trams and this made for a very rigid and durable structure.

Cars 1 - 50. These were conventional four wheel, open top cars built by Milnes; they rode on Brush A trucks of 6ft wheelbase. From 1907 all except car 35 were fitted with top covers with open balconies. Conduit gear was fitted to 25 cars in 1909/10 for through running over LCC lines and this necessitated the lengthening of the truck wheelbase. Cars in this batch were reconstructed by the corporation in the early 1920s. Most survived into LT ownership.

Cars 51 - 85. Delivered in 1905 from Brush, these cars were originally all open top vehicles. Subsequently many were reconstructed with top covers, a few open top cars survived until the late 1920s.

Cars 86 - 93. In 1906 Milnes, Voss and Co. supplied this batch of open top cars which were fitted with 8ft 6ins wheelbase Mountain and Gibson radial trucks. They were all later top covered and reconstructed with the radial gear locked to give a better ride. In 1929/30 upholstered seating was provided in these trams.

Cars 94 - 100. Delivered in 1906, these were top covered cars, with a shorter upper saloon on cars 94 - 97. Their subsequent history mirrored that of cars 86 - 93.

Cars 101 - 106. In 1910 these cars arrived, each having six lower saloon windows and mixed transverse and longitudinal seating. They were fitted with conduit gear and rode on Peckham R7 radial trucks. After reconstruction, the lower saloons reverted to the normal three window arrangement. Car 102 escaped the scrapman and it can now be seen at the London Transport Museum in Covent Garden.

Cars 107 - 118. In 1911 the corporation's first eight wheel bogie cars were delivered. They had open balcony top decks and the lower saloon sported eight windows on each side. In 1922/23 the lower decks were rebuilt with four windows and transverse upholstered seating in the lower saloon was provided in 1926/27.

Cars 119, 60 - 63, 65. In 1923 car 119 was built by the corporation and over the next two years the other trams in this batch appeared. They were the last four wheel trams built for West Ham and they had totally enclosed top decks. Car 119 later became car 64.

Cars 119 - 124. This was a batch of bogie cars with all enclosed top decks. They were built by English Electric and had Hurst Nelson maximum traction trucks. They survived into LT days and three trams were used as staff cars at Charlton Works after the Second World War.

Cars 125 - 137. The first two of this batch were built at West Ham and the rest were delivered by Brush. They were bogie cars with all enclosed top decks and open platforms. They were later fitted with windscreens and many survived into the final months of the London system.

Cars 138, 69 - 85. Car 138 was constructed by the corporation in 1928, to be followed by the others built by Brush. They were equipped with double trolleys and of course conduit gear for working into central London. Most survived in South London until the end in 1952.

Car 68. This tram was built by the corporation in 1931 as an all enclosed bogie car. During the war it was transferred to Abbey Wood Depot and it lived out its remaining days on services 44 and 46.

Car 1A. A water and sweeper car fitted with a 2,000 gallon tank, this works tram was delivered in 1905 and was scrapped early by London Transport.

Car 2A. Smaller than its sister car, this vehicle possessed a 1,200 gallon tank, and it was renumbered 055 by London Transport.

The original livery of West Ham Corporation Tramways was described as munich lake and pale cream. The fleet number on the dash was in gold shaded blue on an orange red background which also formed a diamond shape around the headlamp. The borough coat of arms was displayed on the waist panel of each tram. After the First World War the colours were altered to a rich maroon and deep cream, the maroon has also been likened to a dark plum colour.

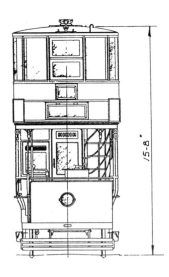

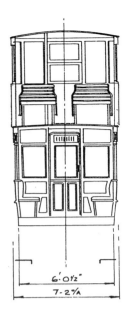

6'·0½"

7'·2⅝"

LONDON TRANSPORT TRAMCAR
ENCLOSED TOP 4 WHEEL CAR

TYPE: EX WEST HAM CORPORATION.
FLEET NO: 272 (W.H. 61-65).   SCALE: 4 mm = 1 Foot

DRAWING No. TC64

SCALE
FEET 0 1 2 3 4 5 6 7 8 9 10 11 12

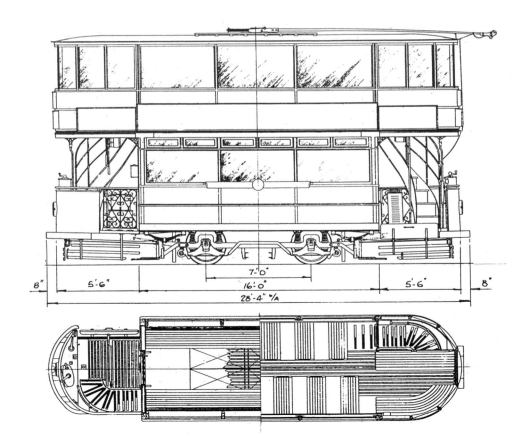

8"   5'·6"   7'·0"   5'·6"   8"
16'·0"
28'·4" ⁰/ₐ

98. In 1905 one of the original West Ham cars was fitted with a Philipson Step and Guard, and it is illustrated here in raised position by the driver and lowered by the conductor. (Tramway and Railway World)

99. Car 20 is shown in its final West Ham condition just after acquisition by LT in 1933. The steps are fixed. (M.J.O'Connor)

100. There is plenty of vintage rolling stock to be seen in this view of Stratford Broadway. LT car 224 is one of the early West Ham cars and 1937 will mark its withdrawal from service. (A.B.Cross)

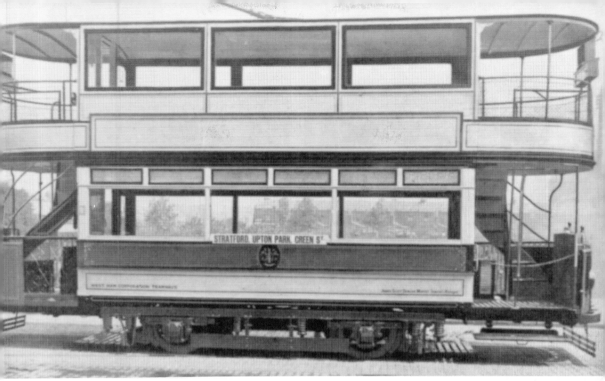

101. The corporation's rolling stock reconstruction skills were described in the Tramway and Railway World in September 1916. This is a side view of car 88 fitted with a new steel frame. (Tramway and Railway World)

102. An end view of car 88 features the service 10 disc above the fleet number, as well as the diamond design round the headlamp. (Tramway and Railway World)

103. Car 92 is typical of the well maintained and smartly liveried fleet in its final days of corporation ownership. (G.N.Southerden)

104. The one that got away! Car 102 is pictured with its original six window lower saloon. This tram was later reconstructed and preserved as a museum exhibit. It is now in the LT Museum at Covent Garden. (UEC works photo)

105. Car 64 was one of the few single truck
vehicles with an enclosed top deck. It is
working circular service 10 which was known
as the cinema tram by the locals, as it passed
just about every picture house in the borough.
(G.N.Southerden)

106. The corporation's first bogie cars had some style about them, but unfortunately they were all ousted by trolleybuses in 1937/38 and did not see further service in South London. (G.N.Southerden)

107. Eight wheel and single truck versions of former West Ham cars demonstrate their final LT red and cream livery. (C.Carter)

108. Car 128 shows the penultimate form of the West Ham bogie car with all enclosed top deck. (M.J.O'Connor)

109. The lower saloon of a refurbished car complete with transverse upholstered seating looks quite comfortable. This was a considerable improvement on the original hard wooden longitudinal benches. (Tramway Museum Society)

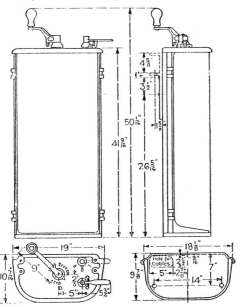

Dimensions of B 49 Controller.

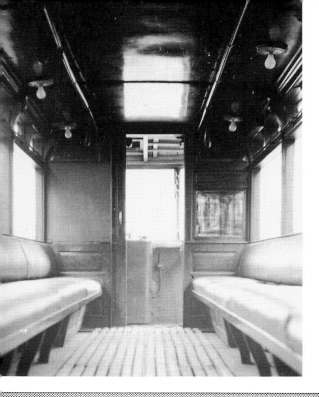

110. LT car 327 ex-West Ham car 121 retained the bench seats in the lower saloon. This tram was used by London Transport as a staff car and could be seen in the final years of the system working from New Cross to Charlton Works. (Tramway Museum Society)

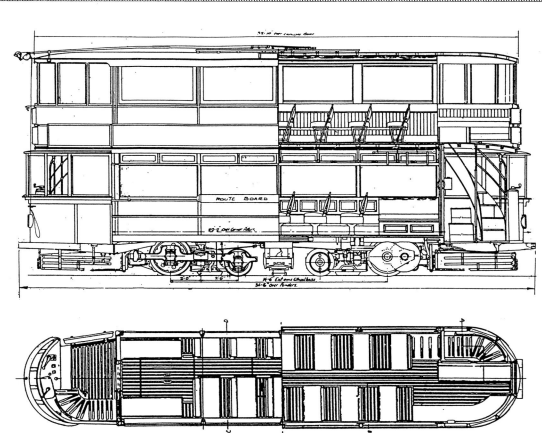

Lower Deck Plan   Upper Deck Plan

111. The interior of the top deck shows the distinctive West Ham end window to the upper saloon. Note also the mirror fixed above the stairwell. (J.C.Gillham)

LONDON TRANSPORT
DOUBLE DECK BOGIE TRAM

TYPE:	SCALE:
EX WEST HAM	4mm = 1 Foot

DRAWING No. TC 261

SCALE FEET 0 1 2 3 4 5 6 7 8 9 10 11 12

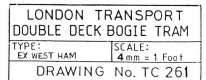

Section A-B

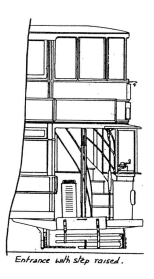

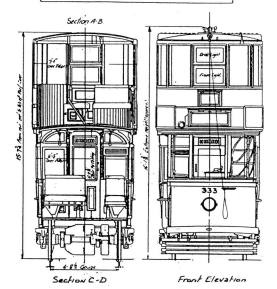

Section C-D

Front Elevation

Entrance with step raised.

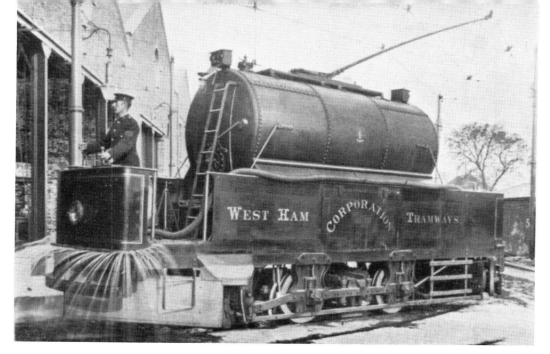

112. Car 68 was the last tram to be built by the corporation and one wonders what might have been, had the transport policy makers in the metropolis pursued a more tramway friendly philosophy. (G.N.Southerden)

113. In the last week of tramway operation in 1952, we observe LT car 312 ex-West Ham car 85 with only a few more days of active service ahead. (J.C.Gillham)

114. Car 1A was equipped with a Mountain and Gibson 5ft 6ins single truck. It demonstrates its cleaning prowess outside the depot. (Tramway and Railway World)

115. Cars 1A and 2A are shown together in the depot forecourt. (Tramway and Railway World)

116. Not all the fleet ran on rails, and here the motorised tower wagon is brought out for the photographer in 1912. The chassis was supplied by Argylls Ltd.
(Tramway and Railway World)

Telephonic Traffic Control For Tramways - The Example Of West Ham..was the title of an article in the Tramway and Railway World for July 1919. The author went on to describe the efficiency achieved by West Ham's use of telephone control points at strategic tramway junctions. The account ended with a copy of a daily traffic report which is reproduced below. Many of the entries remind us of the human side of running a complex transport organisation and of the minor trials and tribulations that were encountered.

DAILY TRAFFIC REPORT.
WEDNESDAY, JUNE 4, 1919.

4.50 a.m.—5.21 a.m.—Current failed on Romford Road, Leytonstone Road, and High Street feeders.

CAUSE.—Defective London County Council car 1153.

LOCALITY OF DELAY.—Bow Bridge to Green Street and Lingfield Road.

SERVICES AFFECTED.—5, 6, 7, 8, 61, and 63.

CARS PROCEEDING TO—Stratford, Canning Town, Wanstead Flats, Docks, Bakers' Arms, Aldgate, Leytonstone, Ilford.

HOW DEALT WITH.—Arriving on duty at 5 a.m., Inspector Clark reported "Current failed at 4.50 a.m. I have been to sub-station to ascertain cause ; sub-station reports no trouble here." Wagon despatched from shed to Stratford. Inspectors Clark, Lawrence, and Wood despatched to inspect lines. The lines reported O.K. The sub-station informed, and instructed to feed until countermanded. Inspector Lawrence to put L.C.C. 1153 in tow for depot. L.C.C. informed by national telephone. Services 5 and 63 turned at Green Street for Canning Town and Ilford. Services 6 and 7 turned at Victoria Street for Canning Town and Docks. One service 8 turned at Adamson Road. On returning, Mr. Somerville informed by Smith.

DELAY.—Thirty-one minutes on one section only.

9.30 a.m.—A breakdown occurred opposite " The Harrow," High Street, Stratford, on the down track. A four-wheeled fish lorry, loaded with fish, owned by Messrs. Blayney and Son, Fishmongers, The White City Fish Shop, Stratford, and in charge of H. Chivers of the same address, the cause of breakdown being due to the off-side front wheel being drawn from the box.

Only a slight delay to traffic. Track in good condition. No complaint made. No police officer present. Mr. Somerville informed, also Claims Department.

10.5 a.m.—A breakdown occurred opposite the Cash Office, Stratford, of a motor and trailer M 6950, owned by Thos. Feast, Cartage Contractor, Silvertown, in charge of George. Lester, 22, Malmesbury Road, Canning Town. The breakdown was due to the collapse of the off-side hind wheel, in bad condition, sample obtained. Trailer loaded with 22 sacks of flour, weighing 2 tons, 15 cwts. Track in good condition, no complaint made. Particulars taken by P.C. 226 K. No delay to traffic. Mr. Somerville and Claims Department informed.

1.35 p.m.—Regulator Young at Plaistow Building reported an accident alleged to have occurred to a Mrs. Emma Eiles, 93, Harcourt Road, West Ham, who complained that she had fallen from a car at Clegg Street, Plaistow, about 12.34 p.m. She has since been to " The Stores." She at first refused medical aid, but afterwards said she would like to see a doctor. She was taken to Dr. Kennedy, Balaam Street, who stated there was no sign of any injury. The car she alleges she fell from is car 53, Service 7, Driver Ellis, Conductor Miller. The conductor denies all knowledge of the accident.

WITHERINGTON.

(Signed) T. SOMERVILLE, Traffic Superintendent.

ALL IN A DAY'S WORK

117. This photograph appeared in the July 1919 article and it shows a tramways official on the phone to the central control room at the depot. In this way help could be summoned immediately in the case of a derailment or service hold up. Also extra trams could be called up to respond to traffic needs. (Tramway and Railway World)

118. Long before the practice of having only one person responsible for a public transport vehicle, the conductor used to perform a vital role. Here we see him supervising people boarding, and amongst his other tasks was the issuing of tickets and general management of the passengers and tramcar whilst the motorman got on with the job of ensuring that all reached their destination safely. (A.B.Cross)

FINALE

119. Trolleybus 1405 has only one trolley pole up at Stratford Broadway. From 1959 onwards all the local trolleybuses were phased out, thus heralding the diesel pollution of the Routemaster bus era. (C.Carter)

No. 264.—TWO-DAY TICKET BOX SYSTEM.

NOTICE TO CONDUCTORS—WEST HAM DEPOT.

Commencing Wednesday, 2nd May, 1934, and every alternate day thereafter, the Conductors' boxes for the West Ham Depot will contain a two-day supply of tickets, with the exception of boxes for use on Sundays, which will provided with a single day supply only.

The special boxes for Sundays will be distinguished from the weekday boxes by blue labels.

WAYBILLS.

A new double day waybill will be provided, but on Sundays a single day waybill only will be issued.

120. Since the trams were double ended they did not need turning circles like this one erected for the new trolleybuses at the Docks terminus in Connaught Road. London Transport admitted the problem of finding suitable loops for trolleybuses and some local side streets were equipped with overhead wires for the replacement vehicles. This scene at Connaught Road now belongs firmly to the past as new roads have changed the face of the area, but on the positive side, the Docklands Light Railway now runs very close to the site and gives clean, quiet transport to this part of London again. (C.Carter)

472.—TROLLEYBUS CONVERSION—WEST HAM, LEYTON AND WALTHAMSTOW AREAS.

Notice to Inspectors and Conductors—West Ham and Walthamstow Depots.

Commencing on Sunday, 6th June, 1937, the following new trolleybus routes will operate :—

669 Stratford and Canning Town as 69 Tram Route.
687 Chingford Mount and Docks as 87 Tram Route.
697 Chingford Mount and Docks as 97 Tram Route.
699 Chingford Mount and Docks as 97 Tram Route to Plaistow Broadway, thence via Prince Regent Lane to Docks.

In consequence Tram Routes Nos. 69, 87, 97 and 99 will be withdrawn and Tram Routes Nos. 55 and 57 curtailed Leyton (" Bakers Arms ") from London.